The Really, Really, Really Useful Series. No.15

PULVI ROYAL

MIKE PEARCE

Copyright 2018 by Mike Pearce

All rights reserved. No part of this book may be reproduced, distributed or transmitted in any form or by any means, including photocopying, recording, or other electronic or mechanical methods, without the prior written permission of the author, except in the case of brief quotations embodied in reviews and certain other non-commercial uses permitted by copyright law. You must not circulate this book in any format.

This book may not be resold or given away to other people. Please respect the work of the author and purchase a copy for you own use.

This is a fictional work and all characters are drawn from the author's imagination. Any resemblance or similarities to persons living or dead are entirely coincidental

DEDICATION

This book is dedicated to all those who wondered what the
white fluffy cotton wool like substance they saw on the
branches of some trees, such as Horse chestnut, limes and
maples was and wanted to know more

CONTENTS

ACKNOWLEDGMENTS

The author would like to thank Christine Pearce
for reading and checking through the manuscript.

PREFACE

Horse chestnut trees can grow to great heights. A joy to those who collect conkers or like a lot of shade. Around the 1960s the horse chestnut scale (Pulvinaria regalis) arrived in this country and began to spread. It liked other trees as well, especially limes and maples.

Local councils and the public soon became aware of Pulvi's presence by the cotton wool like waxy covering produced by these insects along the branches. This story is about one such insect whose short life involved a lot of travelling.

1 MY MOTHER

It is the end of May. My mother lies dead on the branch now. She is just a shrivelled brown disc like scale, rather like rows of Roman shields used in the turtle formation and protected from arrows. She is on the lower branches of my home, a horse chestnut tree in a central London street. She tried to get into depressions in the bark to get the best shelter but never made it. She may be dead but look at her.

The hind side of her thin brown shrunken scale like body is raised at a 45-degree angle forced up by a mass of fluffy wax threads. Inside the threads are tiny glistening cream coloured eggs like eggs in a basket of straw. She sits on her branches next to her many friends who are also dead, a memorial to their presence.

This large number, each with their white waxy egg sacs, makes the branches look as though they are covered in snow and it's only May. I was one of these eggs. The hundreds of eggs she lays ensures that some will survive the destruction that can occur at one point in their life.

They say our ancestors came from Asia in imported plants during the 60s and in a few years were in London. From there they invaded Europe and spread over Europe in the next twenty years. They liked the urban areas. Some say my mother came over on the ferry on top of a coach or car. I know some of us have been transported across the country on the outside of trains. It seemed that a lot of us were found in trees along roads or in car parks, good places for transport to other regions.

My mother was wingless unlike my father. In evolution it was more beneficial and safer for her to be sessile most of the time, increase in size and become an egg laying machine. He also had longer antennae, small and ugly. Unfortunately, he only had a few days to find a partner as he had no mouth parts so could not feed.

However, he was helped by attractive pheromones which my mother released. Her scale when alive, was brown with pale yellow stripes. She had produced her wax sac and eggs in April/May.

2 THE ONSET OF SUMMER

Just before my mother died, I lay there inside this cocoon of fluffy fine wax. The winter was past. We've withstood the ice and frosts which covered the branches of our tree. Showers and sun were becoming more common. The small dormant buds on the trees started to wake up throwing off the bud scales that had protected them. The tree was also taking in minerals and nutrients from the soil and the sap was rising. The small leaves slowly unfurled even at night making ready to get their energy in the day from the sun.

It was time now. The cold months were gone, and we were ready all of us at last to fulfil all our mothers' legacies. I am Pulvi, very small, for someone considered royal (regalis in my name), only just visible to the human eye and extremely light. Once hatched June or July I had to try and crawl out of this waxy web and walk as fast as I could to find a leaf. You can imagine how long my journey could be if I decided to go right to the top of a large horse chestnut tree as many do. I had several others with me, but many would be dislodged, eaten by other insects or trapped in spiders' webs.

I was just about to walk up the midrib of a leaf when the wind blew me high up into the sky. Oh, I travelled up higher with successive gusts and landed on top of a London bus. Here it was difficult to grip the shiny bus surface and I could not walk far. I needed quickly to find a host plant to feed on, another horse chestnut, a sycamore, lime or even some ivy. Luckily many of the lime trees hung over the buses and I was swept up by a branch onto the top of a flat roof at Kensington Mansions.

It was a blackbird that finally put me onto a lime tree. Luckily it didn't eat me. I was attached to its foot as it perched there among the branches singing one of its many songs from its repertoire. I crawled of the foot up to a leaf, but it was covered in sticky honeydew left by aphids. This would be dangerous as the honey dew could attract other insects such as wasps, bees. lady bird larvae and ants. The aphids were between the vein junctions, lots of them. I went back down the leaf stem and climbed up higher. Many of the leaves here were packed with aphids and the leaves below covered in sooty mold fungus. This meant parts of the leaves could die from loss of sap or raised temperature. The mold could also reduce sunlight so that photosynthesis was affected. managing to find a newly emerged leaf without any aphids feeding on it. I settled myself at the edge of a tiny vein and penetrated it with my stylet and started to suck up the delicious sugary sap. I don't know whether this sugary sap was better than that of the horse chestnut tree or not, but it seemed fine by me.

3 A GOOD YEAR

This year was a good year for the tree, plenty of rainfall and sunshine. Each year the tree produced growth rings, the larger ones representing the kind of season the tree had had. They were larger if the season was good and there was better growth.

I was now to sit in this position constantly feeding until September or October. Luckily I have landed on a tree which I am able to feed on. Many of sisters have landed on plants that they cannot feed on because of structural or chemical characteristics. My greenish colour gave me protection and my slightly domed shape helped the rain to run off my back.

It's not that safe sitting on the underside of a leaf being tossed around in heavy winds and pounded by rain. Part of my leaf could be damaged or die or be eaten by some insect. Also, I noticed some of my neighbours had been injected with the eggs of parasitic wasps which would eventually eat out their insides and emerge from their dead bodies. Luckily, so far so good, except for aphids which tried to tap into my plant's feeding line.

So that my breathing tubes on either side of me don't get blocked with dirt from cars, dust or sticky secretions I produce little c shaped, curled wax filaments from glands which have exit pores for the wax rather like the plug hole in a sink. Each piece breaks off and helps protect my breathing passages making them water repellent. Aphids shoot out waste sugary sap from the pair of tubercles near their back ends. I don't have these tubercles but a mouth like exit surrounded by bristles. My sap leaves from here as a ball but doesn't stick to my body as I produce more small segments of wax which adhere to the ball allowing it to fall away from me and down to the ground.

As the year passes the nutrients I receive are diminishing and in a few months the leaves will fall and that would be the end of me. Miss this opportunity then I would be doomed. It's is therefore time to move so I crawl off the leaf and attach myself to small twigs through which I can still feed. Here I will remain through winter until fully grown by the middle of next summer. I may be lucky to find a mate but otherwise, even if not, I can produce viable eggs.

Later I move down onto the side of bigger branches or even the trunk of the tree. I must be careful as some birds would love to eat me. Here I perform my final act. This time it's not small curls of wax I produce but long strands of wax from my hind end. These coil up and become fluffy and sticky. Within these coils I produce my eggs, but I am never, never actually to see my young which is quite sad but they are all part of my royal family and will reign for many centuries to come.

4 WE STILL NEED TREES

Our generations continue year after year. Some years our numbers are many, the branches become as white as snow causing concern to many observers. Other years we can be only a few or on some trees completely absent. This conflict of good and bad years is mirrored in the rings of trees and also in their growth material such as in shellfish and fish scales. One has only to look at wood, carved or sectioned, to see the differences between the years.

These time recorders in wood rings may be visible in furniture made in your lifetime or delve right back to the past and displayed in innumerable shapes and sizes. Each of us links with nature and growth as do the generations of animals that feed on these trees, such as the horse chestnut scale.

As we replace wood by metal and plastic especially

our links with the past dwindle into timeless oblivion

and nature tries to call us back but fails.

To see other publications below by the author visit
snappysnappybooks.com

<u>The really, really, really useful series</u>

How to be a Successful Business Weed
How to Deal with Life's Snakes and Ladders
Know Your Students and Build Your Image
Pens for Pops
How to be a Successful Charity Shop
Make up-revealed
Ronnie's Sermon snippets
Wastefulness-Bone and Urine
Fertility Stones and Chocolate Eggs
Clingers, creepers and scramblers
I Herring Gull
Viking Bay-Natural History
Go Fat Go
Hidden from the heart but not forgotten

<u>Other books by Mike Pearce:</u>

Pattern for Purpose- God's and Man's designs
Red Fred Cell and Friends
Human Termites eat London
Pigeons Splat London
Glass Anemones Tentacle-ize London
Tuppeny Hangover
I am Termite
The littlest Oyster
Bits and Bobs
The Shell Man
Cats at Christmas
Tails, Tales
Trust-Nothing but a Must
In a Dark, Dark Corner was the Holy Ghost
The Shell Lady
Captain Grottbuster versus the Grey World
London's Nemesis (Trilogy of 3, 4 and 5 above
Saved by Angels (Trilogy of 6, 8 and 14 above)
The World of Wax
Photosynthetic Women
Queen Rat on Deadman's Island
The Watcher on the Fal
The Rock Pool
The Little Shepherd Boy's Gift
The Living Fossils
Old Mother Nature Laughed and Laughed

Betty's Barcodes
Time Runs Dry (play)
Valentines Cards
The Scrofula Infirmary
The Cornish Urchin
My Therizinosaurus
Spider in the Tomb
The White Cockerel
The Red Church Doll
Butterfly Angels (compilation of previous books)
The Girl Under the Paeony Tree
Baby Feet
The Sparrows' Last Soul
Ball Rooms
Absorbed by a Woman
St Mildred-Patron Saint of Thanet
The Slothful Wife
The Tuppeny Bear
The Boy who found Christmas
Nothing but leaves
The Giant's Toothpick
The Night Mare
The Old Pot and the Golden Shoes
Sitting next to Angels
Exodus to a leaf
The forlorn fruit fly
The Pawnbroker's Souls
The Nursery Rhyme Cat
A Call Under the Sea
Dead Donkey Lane
A Googolplex of Mice
The Eggstraordinary Easter Egg
The China Blackbird
A slice of Slang with a touch of Cockney and a

drop of Dorset
The Rusty Gate
Beware of Cucumbers, apples and pigs
The Lady loves Red
The woman who smelled books
Till my lips were salt as brine
The Giant and the Giraffe Boy
The man who always sprinted
Boy,could she smell!
Coloured bricks
The Lady who loved Hairspray

ABOUT THE AUTHOR

Dr Mike Pearce is a scientist interested in behaviour. He also was a lecturer in human biology and health at a college in Canterbury, Kent